A Stoic's Approach to News Consumption

How to Stay Informed and Unaffected

Table of Contents

Chapter 1. Introduction

Dive headfirst into a uniquely rewarding journey of mental resilience and insightful understanding of news consumption with our special report, "A Stoic's Approach to News Consumption: How to Stay Informed and Unaffected". In a world exploding with information, staying informed is more important than ever, but so too is maintaining our peace of mind. Come, explore the stoic philosophies that can guide you to absorbing daily news without letting it disrupt your tranquility. Drawing upon ancient wisdom and modern psychology, this report is like a lantern, illuminating a path through the overwhelming forest of 24/7 news cycle. Prepare to revolutionize the way you consume news, maintain your serenity and, ultimately, embrace a more composed and knowledgeable version of yourself. Ready for this empowering transformation? All you need is packed within these pages! Let's get started.

Chapter 2. Introduction to Stoicism and News Consumption

In the digital age where data pervades our lives, it can often be a daunting task to filter relevant news from the incessant flow of information. This feat becomes even more challenging when maintaining one's emotional well-being in the face of negative or overwhelming news is taken into account. A refuge from this seemingly unending struggle can be found in the ancient philosophy of Stoicism. By merging history's lessons, modern life's nuances and psychology's insights, we may discover a more healthy and sustainable way to engage with the pulsating heart of our world - the news.

2.1. Understanding Stoicism

Stoicism, a school of Hellenistic philosophy, was founded in Athens in the 3rd century BC by Zeno of Citium. The philosophy asserts that virtue (such as wisdom) is happiness and judgment should be based on behavior rather than words. The stoics taught that we should strive to maintain tranquility and avoid negative emotions caused by poor judgment. The core of Stoicism lies in differentiating between what we can change and what we can't. By focusing on the former and accepting the latter, we can attain peace and resilience.

The ancient stoics like Marcus Aurelius, Epictetus, and Seneca provide a wealth of knowledge that remains surprisingly relevant today, especially when it comes to managing our emotions while dealing with an ever-changing world. Their teachings focus on self-control, mental fortitude, and clarity of judgment, qualities that we can practice and cultivate to become more resilient.

2.2. Stoicism and Modern Challenges

One of the most significant challenges in the modern world is the abundant information, including news, that we are subjected to every day. Developing a stoic approach to this seeming information chaos can have immense benefits. It can help us sort necessary information from trivial, urgent from non-urgent, and internalize the impact it has on us. It is a skill that requires practice, patience, and the right mindset.

What does it mean to consume news stoically? Essentially, it is about developing a measured and mindful approach, letting logic guide our interpretation and reaction to news. It involves retaining our calm amidst the flood of conflicting narratives and maintaining emotional detachment from the subject at hand to make objective assessments.

2.3. The Intersection of Stoicism and News Consumption

Stoicism and news consumption intersect in an admittedly unusual yet profoundly impactful way. By applying Stoic philosophy, we can learn to approach news mindfully, using it as a tool for enlightenment rather than a source of agitation. For a stoic, news serves to inform and spur thoughtful engagement within their societal context, but not to cause unnecessary emotional turmoil.

2.4. Stoicism's Influence on Perception of News

Stoic philosophy has the potential to substantially change our news consumption patterns. Negative news that tends to invoke panic or fear can be viewed from an analytical lens, avoiding reactionary impulses. Viewing news in a stoic manner doesn't mean becoming apathetic or passive; instead, it encourages us to respond with intentionality and caution, keeping our peace of mind intact.

This philosophy promotes mindfulness about the quality of news we consume. It encourages the pursuit of multiple perspectives before forming judgments, thereby preventing hasty reactions. Taking the time to consume and understand news, while continually checking our emotional responses, aligns perfectly with the stoic ideology of being measured yet engaged citizens.

2.5. Conclusion of The Introduction

Applying Stoicism to our news consumption habits is, in essence, disciplining our mind to become more discerning and dispassionate. Mindful and measured consumption makes us better able to discern misinformation, more resistant to manipulation, and less prone to unnecessary despair. Unleashing the potential of Stoic teachings on our daily reading of a typically frenetic news cycle can revolutionize our relationship with media, leading growth towards a more composed and knowledgeable self.

Our voyage doesn't stop here. The forthcoming sections will provide practical techniques and approaches that will guide you in integrating this ancient philosophy into a modern necessity—news consumption. The transformative quest awaits!

Chapter 3. The Nature of News: Bias, Sensationalism, and Truth

The past several decades have been characterized by an explosion of information. Issues that were once distant and remote are now on our screen, feeding us with an overwhelming amount of information. News is produced and consumed at an unprecedented rate; a continuous stream flowing into our devices, into our lives. This constant intake of news can profoundly influence our tranquillity and peace of mind. Understanding the nature of news is a necessary prerequisite for engaging with it wisely.

3.1. The Evolution of News

The nature of news has not always been as it is today. Over several centuries, news has evolved from an irregularly printed broadsheet or pamphlet intended for a limited audience, to a variety of formats such as newspapers, television, radio, and now digital news. However, the increased accessibility to news is not the only thing that changed. The way news is presented and distributed has also evolved significantly.

Initially, news was presented in a relatively simple, fact-based manner. As media evolved, so did the complexity and intensity of its content. The presentation of news became dynamic, interactive, and not entirely objective. Various factors like commercialization, increased competition and user preferences have contributed to the evolution of news.

Television and later, the internet, revolutionized news consumption. The digitization of news introduced Information Cascades, a phenomenon where information is passed and amplified, often in echo chambers or filter bubbles, leading to a spread of misinformation and bias. Hence, unpicking the inherent biases and understanding the sensationalism embedded in much of today's news coverage is an indispensable step to staying informed and unaffected.

3.2. Unwrapping Bias

Bias in the news is not a new concept, but it has taken on a new dimension in today's digital age. A biased message contains more than the verifiable information; it includes the sender's subjective views, interpretations and personal interests.

Every news outlet is run by humans, who have inherent biases, formed from a complex result of environmental, cognitive, and cultural factors. Further, the outlet itself would be subject to structural bias, resulting from constraints of time, space, and resources, as well as the wider political, sociocultural and economic milieu it operates in.

However, bias is not necessarily bad. By identifying and understanding it, we can build a more nuanced picture of the world. It first requires keen awareness about the existence of biases in the news. Once aware, we can make an effort to actively counteract the impact of these biases, by seeking diverse sources of news and considering different perspectives on the same issue.

3.3. Let's Talk Sensationalism

Often closely related to bias is the concept of sensationalism. Sensationalism, the act of presenting news in a way that provokes public interest or excitement at the expense of accuracy or impartiality, is a commonplace in today's media landscape. It makes news more accessible and exciting but also more alarming and anxiety-inducing. Much like a savory dish using a bit too much salt, the excessive use of sensational elements can overpower the original substance of the news, making it palatable but not exactly wholesome.

Levels of sensationalism have skyrocketed in the digital era, due to the sheer amount of content vying for attention, and the algorithms that prioritize content that generates high engagement. Being aware of the markers of sensationalism – overly dramatic headlines, emotionally charged language, an emphasis on scandal or conflict – can help us respond more judiciously to such news items, reducing their potential to unsettle us.

3.4. Walking Towards the Truth

Despite biases and sensationalism, truth is not completely elusive in the world of news. The crux lies in developing the right skills and perspectives to uncover it.

First, it's crucial to curate a well-rounded media diet, comprising a diverse range of sources covering the entire breadth of the political spectrum. Consuming news from these different sources can help combat bias and provide a more balanced perspective.

Second, develop and exercise critical thinking skills. Evaluate whether the presented facts are credible and verifiable, whether the arguments are well-stated and logical, and whether all aspects of a story are covered. This active engagement with news, rather than passive consumption, can uncover the truth that lies beneath bias and sensationalism.

Understanding the nature of news, the inherent biases, sensationalism, and the path to truth, guides us in dealing with the information avalanche in a stoic manner. As we begin to understand these, we structure our approach to news consumption allowing us to remain informed without it severely affecting our mental peace and tranquility. As we journey through the rest of the report, we will delve deeper into Stoic philosophy and how its principles can aid in dealing with the monolith that is modern news consumption.

This chapter, while appearing daunting, is the foundation. We have now, together, taken an important step towards achieving a harmonious balance between staying informed and staying serene.

Chapter 4. Understanding Stoic Philosophy: The Foundations

Understanding the lessons of stoicism begins with an exploration of its historical roots and core tenets. Originating in Athens around 300 B.C.E., Stoicism was developed by philosopher Zeno of Citium. The philosophy flourished in Greece and later in Rome, influencing many great thinkers such as Seneca, Epictetus, and Marcus Aurelius. Their works have survived millennia and continue to provide profound insights into the human condition and our place in the world.

Stoicism teaches us that we don't always have control over what happens to us, but we do have control over how we respond. In the context of news consumption, this means learning to separate facts from narrative, seeking understanding over immediate reactions, and applying discernment in the face of information overload.

4.1. The Historical Roots of Stoicism

Zeno developed Stoicism after a shipwreck left him in Athens with nothing but the clothes on his back. Finding solace in philosophy, he came to realize that external possessions and events were irrelevant to personal happiness and peace. Thus, he outlined a philosophy oriented towards the inner self, emphasizing emotional resilience and ethical living in alignment with nature's logic.

Roman Stoicism drew heavily on Zeno's teachings, developing them into a robust system that could be practiced anywhere, by anyone. Stoicism became a way of life, transforming individuals and creating leaders of wisdom. Seneca offered profound reflections on life and death; Epictetus, a former slave, framed a philosophical system out of his own experiences; and Marcus Aurelius, a Roman emperor, wrote meditations that served as a personal guide for ethical living and philosophical contemplation.

These ancient stoic texts, while rooted in a vastly different era, remain a wellspring of wisdom for contemporary readers. They provide strategies for cultivating inner peace, making wise decisions, and facing challenges with courage and calmness. Applied to news consumption, this means understanding that while we can't control the news, we can control our responses and interpretations.

4.2. The Core Tenet of Stoicism

One of the core tenets of Stoicism is the essence of control: understanding what we can change and accepting what we cannot. This dichotomy is encapsulated in the famous Serenity Prayer, found in many modern self-help and recovery systems, which is a derivative of the Stoic philosophy.

Epictetus, one of the most renowned Stoic philosophers, taught that we should focus on what is within our power - our thoughts, beliefs, and reactions - while accepting the things outside of our control, such as global events, the actions of others, or the content of daily news. Harnessing and enhancing our energy in the areas we can influence and relinquishing control over externals leads to a more peaceful, content life.

In terms of news consumption, the power of discernment becomes crucial. By focusing not on the events themselves, but rather on our perceptions and reactions to these events, we can avoid becoming emotionally burdened by the incessant hum of the 24/7 news cycle.

4.3. Stoicism and Emotional Resilience

Applied wisely, the principles of Stoicism can solidify our emotional resilience, enabling us to withstand the surge of news without getting pulled under by the current. When we are bombarded by distressing news, we often experience stress, anxiety, and a feeling of helplessness. Stoic philosophy encourages us to examine these feelings and understand that they are not caused by the events themselves but by our judgments about these events.

Marcus Aurelius once said, "If you are distressed by anything external, the pain is not due to the thing itself but to your own estimate of it; and this you have the power to revoke at any moment." This underpins the capacity of stoicism in regulating emotional spikes triggered by news consumption.

By adopting a Stoic approach to news, we choose to embrace a balanced perspective, disallowing a piece of news from overwhelming us. We gain the ability to remain still in a storm, knowing that the tumult resides not in the world outside, but in the perception inside.

Ultimately, Stoicism empowers us with a new lens through which we can view news consumption. This journey into its philosophy is the foundation for developing the skills to stay informed without becoming easily affected by the whirlwind of information we face daily. This understanding is just the first step in a transformation that promises serenity, wisdom, and a fuller appreciation of life's complexities. Our subsequent exploration will delve deeper into concrete strategies and practices of Stoic news consumption, providing actionable advice on fostering discernment, detachment, and intellectual sobriety in the eye of the information storm.

Chapter 5. Balancing Information Intake: Less Is More

In the modern digital age, our life is ceaselessly bombarded with an overload of information, escalating our stress levels and decreasing our ability to make effective decisions. News, for all its virtues of keeping us informed, can be a constant source of this overwhelm. Balancing information intake becomes crucial for mental wellbeing and for optimizing the consumption of news in a meaningful way, which is the focus of our exploration in this segment. The age-old adage "less is more" is surprisingly applicable to modern news consumption. Let's dive into the why and how.

5.1. The Overwhelm of Information Overload

The term 'Information Overload' was first coined by social scientist Bertram Gross in his 1964 piece 'The Managing of Organizations'. His theory is even more pertinent today, almost six decades later. With the advent of the internet, anyone can share information, regardless of its validity, escalating the quantity but not always the quality of content.

Our minds are not equipped to process this constant bombardment of information, leading to a state of overwhelm. Research shows that information overload can result in decreased productivity, impaired decision-making capabilities, and increased stress levels. By observing modes to decrease our intake, we can construct a suitable mechanism to combat this issue, drawing from wisdom both ancient and modern.

5.2. Less is More: Quality over Quantity

The principle of 'Less is More' is a poignant application to news consumption. Highly relevant in a time of 24/7 news cycles, the key to informed yet tranquil knowledge consumption is to regulate the intake and ensure what is read is not only correct but also relevant. Consider the following strategies:

1. Limit your sources: Though the internet is flooded with information platforms, not all are equally reliable. Choose a few trustworthy news outlets and make them your primary information sources.

2. Allocate a specific time: Designate fixed slots for news reading. This not only prevents constant news consumption but also allows you to engage more deeply with the content, leading to a better grasp of the information.

3. Prioritize your topics: Decide what topics are essential to you and focus on them. In-depth knowledge of fewer issues will make you more informed than surface-level knowledge of numerous topics.

5.3. The Stoic Approach to the Problem of Excess

Stoicism offers a profound foundation for managing the excesses of our time. The stoics emphasized focusing on the aspects within our control, urging the dismissal of anything outside of it. For our purpose of improved news consumption, stoics might advise us to use our energy not wrestling with the vastness of information available but choosing how we consume it.

The Stoic philosopher Epictetus, for instance, might suggest treating news akin to the events of our life: dissecting them independently and deciding whether they deserve our attention and emotional investment. Herein lies the quality over quantity debate again. It is far more yielding to engage deeply with fewer stories than to skim through hundreds of them.

5.4. The Paradox of Choice

Choices, in their abundance, can lead to an inability to choose, thereby challenging our mental serenity. Psychologist Barry Schwartz in his insightful work, 'The Paradox of Choice', suggests that reducing choices can greatly decrease anxiety.

Similarly, limiting our news sources and honing down our areas of concern can systematically increase our comprehension of the topics. It also helps maintain peace of mind by reducing the paralysis imposed by the sheer volume of information.

5.5. The 80/20 Principle

Drawing from economist Vilfredo Pareto's 80/20 rule, where 80% of results typically come from 20% of efforts, this principle could also be applied to news consumption. By carefully selecting 20% of news that matters the most and adequately absorbing it can make you more informed than taking in 100% of news superficially.

5.6. The Power of Habits in Information Consumption

Habits frame a significant part of our subconscious actions. Mindful formation of habits pertaining to news consumption can bring about a massive shift in the results. Beginning with building a routine for consuming news at specific times of the day to gradually implementing reading style to focus on information that directly applies to you; these all can shape the way we take in news.

5.7. Conclusion

Balancing information intake is not so much a skill but a discipline that involves recognizing the importance of informed selectivity. By adhering to the valuable advice of ancient Stoic philosophers and modern behavioural economists, we can navigate through the sea of excessive information and anchor ourselves on islands of pertinent knowledge, free from the tumultuous waves of information overload. As we embrace this practice, we'll soon witness a substantial change - a quieter mind, a more focused approach, less stress, and a higher degree of knowledge about the world we inhabit.

In the next segment, we shall explore the role of emotions in news consumption, and how one can master their reactions by applying the tenets of stoicism. Stay tuned, for the journey continues.

Chapter 6. Cognitive Resilience: Stoic Strategies for Emotional Untethering

In the heart of Stoicism lies the crucial premise that we don't have control over external events, but we certainly hold the reins when it comes to our internal states - our perceptions, our responses, and, in general, our mental dialogue.

6.1. The Spectrum of Control

Understanding what is within our control and what is not is the keystone of stoic philosophy. Often, we expend energy on circumstances that lie outside of our sphere of influence, consequently stirring turmoil within our minds. On any given day, news contains an array of global events we have absolutely no control over. And indulging in these pieces of news can trigger emotions of anxiety, anger, frustration, or despair.

By adopting a stoic perspective, we first ascertain our impotence in altering these events. Yet, what we can control is our emotional reaction to the news. Fear, anxiety, or anger in response to news events are mere amplifications of the reality orchestrated by our minds. Stoicism admonishes us to accept the reality without the emotional amplification.

6.2. Building Mental Fortitude

Building cognitive resilience involves developing mental fortitude. Stoics practiced several exercises for this purpose. Let's look at two powerful techniques feasibly integrable into our daily routine.

1. 'Premeditatio Malorum': This technique, translated as 'The Pre-Meditation of Evils' involves contemplating on negative events that could happen. By routinely visualizing worst-case scenarios, we cushion our minds to accept unfavourable news without getting derailed emotionally.

2. 'Practising Discomfort': Living in comfort cocoons us into a sense of false security, a world away from the harsh realities portrayed in the news. Occasionally embracing discomfort - be it through fasting, cold showers, or any form of mild self-denial - strengthens our resilience to adverse news.

6.3. Stoicism and Cognitive Distancing

Stoicism encourages us to practice cognitive distancing, a form of mental step-back to separate ourselves from our immediate thoughts and emotions. This distance provides a space to analyze the emotion, the implicit thought process sparking the emotion, and the rationality (or lack thereof) in such thoughts.

Let's consider the news of a pandemic outbreak. Upon hearing the news, emotions of fear and anxiety may automatically surface. Cognitive distancing helps us identify these automatic thoughts and analyze the underlying assumptions. Are all pandemics deadly? What preventive measures can I take? Contemplating these questions challenges our irrational fears, helping us better manage our emotions.

6.4. Stoic Journaling: The Power of Reflective Writing

Stoicism advocates the habit of journaling as a recourse to introspection. It acts as a mirror reflecting our thoughts and emotions. These reflections serve to rationalize emotions that news often evokes.

While encountering a potentially fear-inducing news article, jot down the immediate thoughts and feelings associated with it. Analyze these entries at a later time when the immediacy of emotional response has subdued. The intent is to understand the thought-emotion link and debunk any irrational thoughts provoking uncontrolled emotional responses.

6.5. Conclusion: Emotional Untethering through Stoicism

In a world where we're constantly bombarded with news, it's easy to get emotionally entangled. By practising stoicism, we slowly cultivate the skill of emotional untethering. We begin to realize that news is purely informational - devoid of emotional charge, and our reactions are based on our internal interpretations.

Remember, developing cognitive resilience is a gradual process - akin to training a muscle. Over time, with consistent practice of Stoic techniques discussed here, our cognitive resilience towards news consumption will significantly improve. We will evolve into better-informed, more peaceful individuals who can factually absorb news information while remaining emotionally unscathed. And that is the epitome of stoic mastery.

Chapter 7. Sifting Fact from Fiction: A Stoic's Guide

In the world of perpetual news, it can feel like wading through a flood. To help navigate these waters, we need to start at the most important point: discerning fact from fiction. This ability is undoubtedly one of the essential steps in transforming the way we consume news. The Stoics are our guides, their philosophy a practical method that can be deployed to carry out this task.

7.1. Dissecting the News: The Stoic Way

Stoics perceived the world in terms of what is within our control and what is not. Thus, when it comes to news, we ought to seek factuality first and foremost, realizing that individuals and organizations presenting the news may have biases or intentions beyond simple transmission of information.

The starting point lies in understanding that several news sources often have an inherent bias. It does not make them untrustworthy, rather it calls for approaching them with a dose of healthy skepticism.

7.2. Mindful Selection of News Sources

Be intentional in choosing where you get your news from. Opt for sources known for their factual objective reporting. Organizations that adhere to journalism ethics and standards are commonly better choices. Be aware, multiple sources should be preferred to counterbalance any inherent bias.

Cross-verifying news from different sources can be a useful tool in finding the facts. Much like the philosophy of Stoicism calls for clear, objective evaluation of self and the world, cross-verification mandates the news consumer's objective evaluation of headlines and stories.

7.3. Seeing Through the Spin

News is a realm where spin-doctors are omnipresent, twisting facts to cater to a certain narrative. Here, our power lies in refusing to immediately accept what we're told and instead question, investigate, and evaluate.

Imploring the lens of skepticism against prevalent narratives can be highly beneficial. This stoic tool aids in the careful examination of information fragments, underpinning the true from the misleading.

7.4. The Emotional Guardrail: Avoiding Emotional Manipulation

Emotions are powerful tools for manipulation. Sensational news often plays on fear, anxiety or anger to draw viewers in. A stoic approach demands objectivity, challenging the viewers to see past these emotional narratives.

Using emotional awareness as a guardrail is essential. Be aware of your emotions while consuming news. Understanding that news, especially sensational stories, aim to elicit strong emotions can be your first line of defense against manipulation.

7.5. Logic is Your Ally

Last but not least, employ logic. Factual information may appear as mere drops in the ocean of news content, and it is through logical inquiry we can hope to distinguish them. With solid deductive reasoning, we can dissect news stories, separate fact from fiction, and ultimately, form a balanced perspective.

Much like Stoicism encourages the exercise of logic, we too need to employ it in our consumption of news. Look for the trail of evidence. Where does the information originate, and has it been relayed accurately? How many sources confirm this scenario? What do experts on the matter say?

7.6. Conclusion: The Path Forward

Being a stoic consumer of news, at first, may seem like an insurmountable mountain. However, with practice, you'll find that these practical steps help you sift fact from fiction and allow for a healthier, more balanced approach to news consumption.

Like stoicism itself, it is not about perfection but progression. Changing our consumption habits is a journey, something we improve on bit by bit, day by day. It begins with an intent to change and continues with each news article we read.

The Stoic approach can radically transform our relationship with the news. It enables us to stay aware and informed, but without the stress, anxiety, or anger often stirred up by the round-the-clock news cycle. In the end, it brings us closer to attaining tranquillity while staying connected with the world around us.

Chapter 8. Decoding Sensationalism: Learning to See Beyond the Hype

Modern news distribution - be it the 6 o'clock television broadsheet, or the social media tweet - is becoming increasingly sensationalist. Admittedly, it's a difficult landscape to navigate. We're constantly bombarded with dramatic headlines designed to grab attention and incite emotional reactions, but often at the cost of explicit context and detailed content. How, then, can we see beyond this hype? Awareness and understanding are our first steps.

8.1. Sensationalism Defined

Sensationalism, in a nutshell, can be defined as the use of shocking details or sensational language to provoke a quick, strong, and typically superficial emotional response from the audience. It's not new. It made its way into journalism in the 19th century as newspapers competed for readership, peppering their pages with scandalous and exaggerated stories. With the advent of digital media, sensationalism found its perfect breeding ground. Speed became paramount as outlets vied to be the first to break a story, often compromising accuracy and nuance in the process.

However, the Stoic reserves judgement until comprehending the entire scenario, remembering always that it's our responses to circumstances, rather than the circumstances themselves, that cause emotional upheaval. Let's delve into how to utilize this stoic principle in our consumption of news.

8.2. The Art of Detached Observation

A core tenet of stoicism is maintaining a level of detachment that empowers you to observe situations without getting emotionally involved. By applying this principle to news consumption, you can learn to observe the news as an uninvolved party and question the narrative that's being presented.

Critically question the information presented: is the language filled with powerful but vague words designed to invoke an immediate response? Is it leaning on dramatic imagery or anecdotes over cold-hard facts? How reliable is the source? Take nothing at face value; instead, distance yourself from the story, focusing only on what is factual and ignoring the sensationalist noise surrounding it.

8.3. Digging Deeper for Balance and Context

No news story exists in a vacuum. Every event is part of a larger scenario or a deeper issue. Sensationalism often overlooks this context, focusing instead on isolated incidents that incite immediate emotional reactions. As stoics, we must not let immediate reactions cloud our judgement and must look for balance and context instead.

Dig deeper by cross-referencing information from multiple sources. This will help get a more balanced view and frame the story in its correct context. Avoid drawing conclusions based on information from a single source. Instead, try to understand the bigger picture by connecting the dots independently.

8.4. Understanding the Role Emotions Play

It's important to remember that news organizations have a vested interest in inciting our emotions. More emotion-driven engagement means more clicks, more advertising revenue, and higher profits. Acknowledge this dynamic, take note of it, and use it to inform your understanding of the news.

A stoic approach calls us to be aware of our emotions, but not controlled by them. Consider your emotional response to a news story critically. Are you responding to the core facts or the sensationalist presentation? This awareness can help separate emotionally-charged reactions from rational responses.

8.5. The Power of Pausing Before Reaction

Frenzied, 24/7 news cycles encourage immediate reactions. The stoic, however, understands the importance of patience and clear thinking in maintaining inner peace. When confronted with a sensational piece of news, force yourself to step back, to pause. Stay silent, ruminate on the information, and let your mind process it.

The present is often filled with emotional turbulence. By pausing before reacting, you give the mind time to settle. It's much like stirring a glass of water filled with sediment – the more you stir, the more agitated it becomes. Stop the stirring and everything begins to settle.

In conclusion, seeing through sensationalism involves developing a keen eye for distinguishing facts from hype, understanding the context within which every story operates, and maintaining emotional equilibrium despite attempts to disrupt it. Remember, like any skill, it requires consistent practice. It won't take long before you find yourself consuming news with the calm and rational thinking championed by stoicism, navigating the informational onslaught with a composed mind and a discerning eye.

Chapter 9. Practical Stoic Exercises for News Consumption

News consumption can be a taxing exercise, not only absorbing our time but also, on occasions, weighing heavy on our psyche. Pulling from the deep reservoirs of stoic philosophy and recent advancements in cognitive behavioral therapy, let's equip ourselves with practical tools to navigate news consumption in a healthier, more effective way.

9.1. Constructing a Stoic Anchor

Before delving into active exercises, let's first establish a stoic anchor. This anchor must be an axiom, a principle you hold dear and that can muddle the roughest of emotional storms. The cornerstone of this axiom can be derived from Epictetus's Enchiridion, "People are not disturbed by things, but by the views they take on them."

With this at your core, understand that no news in itself is sufficient to disturb you. It is only your interpretation and consequent emotion attached to it that has the potential to disrupt your peace.

9.2. Analyze Rather than Absorb

Reacting to news impulsively is easy and usually the norm. Stoicism nudges us to analyze instead of absorbing everything passively. Stoics recommend us to employ our reason, our highest faculty, in our approach to the news. In practical terms, this means forming the habit of questioning the source, context, implications, and biases before forming an opinion.

This stoic practice called 'distancing' encourages critical thinking and prevents us from being submissive consumers of information, helping us to maintain an emotional equilibrium even in the face of disturbing events or news pieces.

9.3. Reflection before Reaction

An important stoic principle is to divide events into what is in our control and what is not. Reflecting and discerning between the two before reacting can make a sea of difference to our mental state.

When a piece of news crosses our path, the stoic principle advises first understanding and reminding ourselves that the actual event reported is beyond our control. Next, one should focus on what lies within our control i.e., our reaction to it.

This exercise of reflection ensures that we don't let external events influence our peace, staying grounded and unaffected by the constant turbulences of the outer world.

9.4. The View from Above

A powerful stoic visualization exercise, 'The View from Above' helps broaden our perspective to see the bigger picture. This involves visualizing oneself rising above - looking at our planet from space, seeing nations without borders, recognizing universal human striving and struggles.

This exercise, when applied to news consumption, allows us to contextualize the events, giving us a clearer perspective. This clarity further helps in diffusing strong emotions associated with the news, allowing us to respond rather than react.

9.5. Reclaiming the Power of Attention

In an era where every piece of news competes for our attention, it becomes imperative to make thoughtful choices about where we focus. The Stoic exercise of voluntary self-denial allows us to consciously decide what merits our interest.

If certain news pieces consistently cause distress, question their usefulness for your life and well-being. Limiting exposure can help maintaining mental balance. But remember, this is not about avoiding reality, it's about ensuring that you're consuming news in a healthy and balanced way.

9.6. Keep the End in Mind

'Starting with the end in mind' is an effective stoic exercise while dealing with news consumption. Each time you sit down to consume news, remind yourself of the end goal - to stay informed, not stressed or overwhelmed.

This small mental reminder before diving into the news can support awareness and mindfulness. It acts as a sobering filter, helping you to sift chaff from the wheat, guiding you towards more balanced, objective news consumption.

Practicing these exercises can render news consumption a nourishing, enlightening experience rather than a distressing activity. These steps are not a one-off trick, but a way of life - a stoic life that is rewarding, resilient, and reflective. As with all practices, consistency is key. So arm yourself with these stoic shields, and fight off the stress associated with news consumption. Led by the light of stoicism, cultivate a well-informed yet serene mind.

Chapter 10. Maintaining Tranquility in Turbulent Times: Stoic Lessons

Finding tranquility in today's world can feel as elusive as finding an oasis in an endless desert. This overwhelming sentiment is exacerbated by the constant bombardment of news, sensational headlines, urgent alerts, and viral narratives. In such turbulent times, the teachings of Stoicism, an ancient Greek philosophy, come as a refreshing beverage, quenching our thirst for peace. Stoicism can help you regain your lost tranquility by guiding you to control your reactions, intentions, and ultimately, your sense of wellbeing.

10.1. The Ground Principle: Differentiate Between What You Control and What You Do Not

The core tenet of Stoicism is understanding the difference between things you can control and things you cannot. The stoic philosophers Epictetus succinctly stated, "We control our reasoned choice and all acts that depend on that moral will. What's not under our control are the body and any of its parts, our possessions, parents, siblings, children, or country—anything with which we might associate."

In terms of news consumption, it means recognizing that events happening worldwide are beyond your control. You cannot alter the course of political events, stop earth-shattering disasters, or sway public opinion singlehandedly. But what you control is your attitude towards such news, your decision to consume it, how much you consume, and how you let it affect your emotions and thoughts.

Practice reminding yourself of this principle repeatedly. Make a mental or physical note whenever you come across a piece of news causing emotional distress: "Can I control it?" If not, then acknowledge the feeling aroused but also let it pass. This habit helps in maintaining distance from emotional turbulence caused by uncontrollable events.

10.2. News Consumption: Become an Observer, Not a Participant

One efficient way to consume news in a stoic way is to approach it as an observer—gathering information, understanding the situation, but not indulging in emotional turmoil. Consider yourself a bird soaring high above, watching the events on the ground without getting entangled in them.

You need not suppress your feelings entirely—acknowledge them but do not let them overpower your tranquility. This trains your mental resilience to withstand the onslaught of dramatic news and intense social media dialogue. Keep reminding yourself, "I am an observer, not a participant."

By practicing this, even upsetting news will have limited impact on your tranquility. You will become a stoic news consumer, whose mental state isn't influenced by the turbulence in the news.

10.3. Selecting News: Shield Yourself with Mental Gatekeeping

Maintaining an indifferent observer's stance does not require indulging in all news indiscriminately. Say no to sensational news channels, social media feeds brimming with unverified information, emotional news articles, or biased viewpoints. It's crucial to remember you have the power to choose what information you receive.

The stoic emperor Marcus Aurelius once said, "Today I escaped anxiety. Or no, I discarded it, because it was within me, in my own perceptions — not outside."

You control the gates to your mind; hence you have the command to let in well-reasoned, neutral perspective news or biased, sensational one. Practice this mental gatekeeping and discard anxiety-provoking sources.

10.4. Mindfulness: Be in the Present

Stoicism encourages living in the present moment—imperative advice for news consumers. Frequently, news dredges up stories from the past, and speculates about the future. While analyzing history or pondering future implications is useful, it becomes unhealthy when it torments your mind and steals your present peace.

Needless worries about past events and anxiety about future occurings can disrupt your tranquility. Practice mindfulness. Be in the present. When you consume news, take it as an update of the present moment. Do not let it pull you into the past or push you towards an uncertain future.

10.5. Developing Indifference: Practice Apatheia

In stoicism, 'apatheia' refers to a state of mind where one is indifferent to things one has no control over. By developing 'apatheia,' you reduce the chance of your tranquility being disrupted by tumultuous news.

This does not advocate becoming insensitive or uncaring but rather exercising selective indifference—being concerned about things under your control and indifferent to those which are not. Imagine being like a tranquil sea, unmoved by storms raging in the distance.

10.6. Fortitude: The Final Destination

The culmination of all the practices detailed above is the development of fortitude. Fortitude is mental and emotional strength in the face of adversity. By practicing stoicism in your news consumption, you will build a robust fortress of fortitude, impervious to the barrage of news that threatens your tranquility.

Remember, the journey towards tranquil news consumption isn't a swift sprint but a marathon. It may be challenging initially, yet with practice, you will refine these stoic strategies, gradually noticing an increase in your mental resilience and a more tranquil state of mind. Your stoic approach to consuming news will shield your peace and pave the way to inner tranquility, even in the most tumultuous times. As Seneca, the stoic philosopher, encouraged: "Brave without ceasing: in the smallest matters no less than in the greatest, let magnanimity display itself."

Chapter 11. A Stoic's Reflection: Toward Mindful and Counter-emotional News Consumption

Understanding the world around us, especially in relation to news consumption, is no small task. It requires us to dissect difficult topics, wade through a swirl of facts and perspectives, and then form our own conclusions. In this chapter, we will explore how adopting a stoic mindset, characterized by wisdom, courage, justice, and moderation, can help us navigate the modern news landscape while maintaining our inner peace.

Before we embark on the journey of blending stoicism with news consumption, let's take a moment to recognize the importance of stoicism itself. Stoicism, originating from the Hellenistic period, is a philosophy centered around the cultivation of virtue and wisdom as key components to achieving tranquility. It encourages the recognition and acceptance of what is within our control and what is not.

11.1. The Philosophy of Stoicism

A founding principle of stoicism is understanding and accepting the things that we can't control. The news is a perfect example of this, as it primarily consists of things happening outside of our individual control. However, what we can control is how we react to the news and interpret it.

To gain a deep understanding of this stoic technique, we must first delve into the basics of stoic philosophy. Stoics like Epictetus and Marcus Aurelius believed that our primary task in life is to determine and distinguish between what is up to us and what is not up to us. Only our own judgments, motivations, desires, aversions, and, in sum, our internal responses to external events, are up to us.

11.2. Applying Stoicism in News Consumption

When applied to news consumption, the primary takeaway from Stoic philosophy is this: We cannot control the events that happen in the world and are reported in the news. However, we can control our reactions and judgements to these events. Instead of allowing news to spark fear, anger, or frustration, we can decide to approach news with equanimity and wisdom.

However, this does not mean to be indifferent to the world affairs; we should still maintain an informed perspective. But we can do it without embedding ourselves emotionally. Counter-emotional news consumption does not mean being uncaring or dismissive but means fostering a calm demeanor that helps us perceive news more objectively.

11.3. The Importance of Mindfulness

Mindfulness plays a crucial role in this stoic approach to news consumption. The concept of mindfulness, while it originates from Buddhist meditative traditions, aligns well with Stoicism. A core facet of both philosophies is the emphasis on awareness and presence in the moment.

Mindful news consumption involves being fully present while consuming news, intentionally directing our attention to content without allowing distractions or preconceived notions to cloud our understanding. Instead of passively scrolling news headlines, we engage actively, taking the time to understand the details, and before reacting, we reflect on why we're reacting.

This practice does not come spontaneously; it requires consistent effort. However, with time it becomes a natural way of news consumption, leading to more clarity and less stress.

11.4. Techniques for Mindful News Consumption

Incorporating stoicism and mindfulness into news consumption requires tangible techniques and strategies. Here are a few to start with:

1. Limit news consumption: Allocate specific times during the day for news consumption instead of being constantly connected.

2. Analyze before reacting: Before formulating an opinion, dissect the information, recognize its sources, and compare multiple viewpoints.

3. Practice emotional resilience: Recognize your emotional responses to certain news and question why you're having those reactions. By understanding and controlling our emotions, we can approach news more objectively.

11.5. Cultivating Emotional Resilience

In line with the Stoic principles, one of the most significant aspects of this mindful approach is fostering emotional resilience. This doesn't mean suppressing emotions. Instead, it involves acknowledging emotions, understanding their source, and rationalizing if they're just reactionary or truly aligned with your beliefs.

Every time we encounter news that triggers strong emotions, it's an opportunity to practice emotional resilience. It is about remaining steady within the storm, acknowledging our emotional response while not letting it cloud our judgment.

11.6. Conclusion: News Consumption for the Stoic

In this chaotic world where news is constantly thrown our way, having a stoic approach to news consumption lets us stay in control. This practice not only allows us to understand the world around us in a balanced way but also to maintain our emotional and mental health.

A mindful and counter-emotional approach towards news doesn't negate the importance of staying informed or dampen the quest for truth. Rather, it allows us to absorb information objectively, analyze it from a vantage of calm, and then act or respond, if needed, from a place of wisdom and stability instead of a reactive emotion.

With consistent practice, this Stoic inspired approach to news consumption can revolutionize our engagement with news, leading to more knowledgeable and composed selves. It instills a sense of power, knowing we can control our reaction to the world events, thereby maintaining our tranquility amidst the chaos. This is just one of the ways the age-old wisdom of Stoicism is still tremendously applicable in our lives today.

www.ingramcontent.com/pod-product-compliance
Lightning Source LLC
Chambersburg PA
CBHW060855260726

48661CB00008B/3284